101 Ways to Make Money Taking Photos: Learn How to Get Paid for Pictures and Create Your Own Photography Job!

by Kiara Leigh

Introduction

For amateur photographers, the art of photography is about the fun of capturing an image with the shutter, trying to replicate what you see or even create something new.

The challenge is in the hunt to get the photo, and the thrill is in showing it off to friends and family or even just privately relishing it.

If you've never contemplated the idea of getting paid for your writing before, it might seem thrilling or scary.

If you are confident in your skills, some of these tips involve working with others, while if you don't feel ready yet, others involve selling your work that you have already done.

Consider all these tips jumping-off points – there isn't enough information here to launch a business without further research, but these are all viable ways of making extra money or even forming a business.

Get your brain working over these ideas, thinking about ways to make money with your passion, and you might be surprised at what you come up with. Happy shooting!

1: Learn from the greats

Study great photos to learn the basics of style, form, lighting, etc.

Before you begin to make enormous profits from your photos, you need to know how to take decent photos.

Even if you already take great photos, you can probably improve.

Consider purchasing instructional photo books that include examples of famous photographs and what makes them "work" so well.

Photography classes are also available if you don't know enough about the terminology to do this yourself.

Time spent improving can pay off big-time.

2: Take tourists' photos

They want to see pics of themselves in the tacky tourist haunts nearby you.

You might hate having tourists traipsing through your local spots, but why not profit from them instead?

If you have a historical destination, cultural hotspot or tourist haunt nearby that everyone likes being photographed in front of, set yourself up and take pictures of tourists.

You could charge a few dollars and take pictures with their cameras, or bring along your own camera and a photo printer for more money.

As long as you don't get kicked out by officials, you can make a killing by catering to tourists' needs and meeting cool people.

3: Be a paparazzo

You might get punched in the face, but at least you can make money from it.

This works best if you're in a celebrity hotspot, or if you have a few well-known celebs who like to vacation nearby. Look up celebrity hotspots online and do your best to be there when they are.

You need to know who's who, as they won't always be obvious (so they can avoid you).

Try to capture them doing something more than grocery shopping. Whether that's making out in a club or buying cigarettes when they claimed they'd quit, fighting with the ex or kicking the dog, get pics of it.

You can sell the juicy photos and story to agencies or tabloids if you want to profit.

4

4: Take pics of their junk

People like to sell things on eBay, but few can take good pics of their stuff.

If you know friends, families or neighbors who sell on eBay, you're off to a good start.

You can also advertise your stellar photography services on eBay, Craigslist, or even with flyers on bulletin boards.

Take a good number of sample pictures of various products you have lying around your home, and make them all as professional as possible. Learn how to do this if you don't already know! Backdrops, lightning and details make the difference.

You can charge a flat fee for a set of product pictures, or a percentage of sale if you prefer (go this way with big-ticket items).

5: Help people find love

People need attractive pictures of themselves to attract their soulmates.

No matter what you think about a society that judges people on looks, there's no doubt that attractive profile pics can make the difference between failure and success on dating sites.

Works best in big cities, obviously, but even if you have a few hundred people in your town on various dating sites, it could work.

Advertise on dating site forums, in the community, and through word-of-mouth referrals.

Take a set of photos that include poses, natural outdoors pics, and more. Have fun and get them to relax and smile!

6: Snoop around houses

Real estate agents and 'for sale by owners' need good pictures of homes.

You can get in contact with local real estate agents and ask if they need freelance house photographers, or advertise on FSBO websites and local bulletin boards. It's a good living if you know what you're doing.

Practice by taking photos of your own house or friends' houses, and ask experienced photographers what works.

You want to make the photos clutter-free, as spacious as possible, and show as much as possible. This can involve moving furniture or cleaning up after people sometimes.

The more practice you get, the better you'll know what makes a great set of home pics.

7: Find a good Santa

Maybe a friend has a Santa costume or can rent one; split the profits.

Everyone wants photos of their kids with Santa, and not everyone wants to wait in the noisy, crowded shopping malls to get them.

Set up a studio at home, in a trailer, or outdoors if you can find a scenic park and advertise like crazy.

Even a Christmas tree or snow-covered boughs in the background can be festive enough.

Get a friend who likes kids and stifling costumes to play Santa while you take pictures, and the two of you can split the profits 50/50. For bonus points, find a Mrs. Claus too and take "Claus sandwich" pics!

8: Befriend animals too

Pet owners want pretty pictures of Fido or Fluffy. Bandaids optional.

If you like animals and you're patient, you could make good money taking photos of peoples' beloved pets. Not for the faint-hearted, as sometimes Fido is a little more aggressive than the owner will admit.

Set the animals up outdoors or in an uncluttered room, surround them with blankets and toys, and take a ton of photos.

Animals don't like staying still, so try to arrange to take photos of them around their usual nap-time, or play soothing music.

Partner with a pet-grooming salon or doggie daycare to find built-in clients and improve both of your businesses at once.

9: Religion pays off

Document bar/bat mitzvahs, christenings, and other ceremonies.

Many religions have some form of ceremony as a child is baptized, christened, or somehow initiated into the religion.

Depending on the predominant religions in your area (do some research if you don't know), this could involve a lot of baby photography, moody preteens, and there will usually be fussy grandparents around.

If you love people and are openminded about different religious practices, you could find this fascinating and help people to preserve their special memories too.

Ask churches and places of worship about photographing these events.

10: Here comes the bride

Wedding photos cost a lot; learn to do them and you can charge that, too.

If you're confident in your skills as a portrait and event photographer, cool-headed enough to deal with Bridezilla, and able to best pals with the groom in five minutes flat, wedding photography might be for you.

Don't bill yourself as experienced if you aren't, because there's only one chance to get this right and you don't want to let customers down.

Learn the "essential" wedding photographs (certain people always get included in certain photos), practice at friends' cheap fly-by-night weddings (or with another photographer). Give the couple a wedding album, CD, and prints for best satisfaction.

11: Take headshots

Professionals often need these types of pictures cheap and fast.

Not just actors and models, but professionals of all types need headshots for resumes, company brochures, and all sorts of odd uses.

If you set up an easily portable studio with a backdrop, lighting, tripod, camera and stool, you can take headshots anytime people call in an emergency needing them by tomorrow.

Don't charge a fortune, because this isn't modeling. Look up guidelines on popular types of headshots (models, CEOs, etc).

Sometimes, people just want their headshots as prints, while others might want the .jpg files. Consider charging different prices.

12: Family portraits

These can be a nightmare or a lot of fun. Holiday season pics are popular.

If you were ever subjected to a family portrait session with a dull photographer, you know how much a family loves a great, friendly, professional family portrait photographer.

You could have repeat business for years if you treat your customers right.

Don't rush them, take many shots to give them a lot of choices, and consider throwing in a few free bonus shots, or a silly one for giggles.

You could even turn it into a sketch or add a watercolor effect with Photoshop or another program and include that for bonus value.

13: Do boudoir photos

Help ladies (and gents) give a unique Valentine's Day or Christmas present.

Not for everyone, but sometimes, a lady (or gent) might want to give a loved one a provocative present.

You don't want to be caught by said loved one and accused of anything, so be careful to stay professional at all times and don't treat the person as a lifeless model.

Spend time getting to know the person and their personality before deciding how to do the photos. One lady might be the perfect personality for some pin-up kitchen pics, while another is the bedroom photo sort.

Maintain customer confidentiality at all times and never show others these pics.

14: Decorate a café

Small cafés and coffee shops need art, and you need eyes on your work.

Offer framed or matted prints of your photography to small, independent coffee shops and cafés that don't have a home office dictating what they should hang on their walls.

They need some ambiance and possible conversation pieces, while you need people to see your work and perhaps purchase it.

Let the coffee shop display your work for free. In exchange, your name, phone number and the price of the piece should be prominently displayed on a tag on the bottom of the picture.

Win-win situations make everyone happy.

15: Make fridge magnets

Use the internet to sell magnets and spruce up fridges with your photos.

There are plenty of websites that allow you to sell custom photo magnets.

Choose your best animal, landscape, architecture, or people photographs and upload them to the sites, then let people buy these magnets.

You could also print them yourself if you know how and sell them at craft fairs. Include your name and number on the back.

If you're really bold, go to stores that sell fridges (small appliance stores are the best) and offer them a portion of the profits if they sell your magnets to customers who buy fridges.

16: Personalize items

From mousepads to coffee mugs, people like to decorate their stuff.

Similar to the idea above, there are many items that you can personalize using websites that allow you to upload your own photos.

If you have a photo printer and know how to use it, you could bring it, some premade blank items, and your camera to a craft fair and take pictures of people or kids, print them on the objects, and sell them.

Either way, you get your name out there and make people happy by customizing their stuff.

These make great gifts for Christmas, birthdays, and even Valentine's Day.

17: Be a calendar girl/boy

Maybe you don't want to be in one, but you can make your own calendar.

You can make themed calendars for any interest or taste. For example, a cat calendar might interest little old ladies, while a calendar with snake pictures could captivate kids.

Sell them anywhere you want – online, at a craft fair, or to coworkers.

If you know how, create custom calendars with thirteen or more pictures (one for the cover) of people's families, homes or lives. This sentimental gift will keep giving all year long.

Find groups of themed but unique pictures and look up calendar printing websites.

18: Record your travels

If you get good enough, you can be paid to travel around the world!

Start by documenting an area nearby you and submit to publications either locally or abroad that have an interest in your area.

If you go on vacation, take advantage of it to take some less personalized pictures (editors don't want pics of you and your kids) and more generic photos like the architecture, landscapes, animals, etc.

This has great potential to repay you for the cost of the trip and maybe even more.

Once you have your first publication credits, you can even approach international magazines and offer to do a laser-targeted story about a particular interest or area.

19: Be a guru to others

It's fun to share what you know, and more fun to watch students succeed.

If you have a solid knowledge of the basics of photography, why not teach others?

Now that everyone and their uncle has a digital camera, media is in the hands of consumers... but not all consumers know how to use them.

Provide an alternative to expensive photography classes and teach seniors, adults or kids how to take photos. Hold beginner, intermediate and advanced classes depending on your own skill level.

You can even have a contest among your students and pay a small prize to the winner from the earnings you made from tuition.

20: Sell stock photos

The most overrated way of making money, but this does have potential.

You probably already know about this method, and may have even tried it yourself. If so, you know that the hype isn't true.

You can't sell most pictures you already have on your hard drive, and it takes work and luck to compose good stock photos.

However, if you have the patience to experiment and find out what works (hint: most publications don't need another sunset or landscape photo), this can pay off handsomely.

For success, submit your best photos (not every single one) and keep submitting a steady stream of them over time.

21: Be known in a niche

Maybe you love roses, cars, or old buildings. Become an expert at it.

There is a lot of potential in niches.
Everyone can "take pictures" of anything, but not everyone can become known as the best car photographer in the area.

If you have a particular passion for an object or event, turn yourself into a niche photography expert by practicing taking pictures of that thing... a lot.

It takes hard work to become an expert, but if your niche is small enough, you could find yourself the only one, meaning you get contacted by people, media, and companies who really need an expert.

22: Be a comic artist

Photo comics, or fumetti, are becoming a popular genre of web comic.

If you can tell a story with pictures and a few words, making people laugh or pointing out some irony that exists in society, you might enjoy doing this.

It's more of a hobby than a paid profession, but you can turn it into a money-maker by building up fans, releasing a book of comics or merchandise, or monetizing a comic website with Adsense or other offers.

You'll need to have a good knowledge of comic creation (this may mean a lot of practice and time put into it), but as far as fun things go, this makes the list.

23: Be a capitalist

Political beliefs aside, capitalize on streams of income that already exist.

This is simple: take what works and expand it. Make more money from streams of income you already have going.

If you sell wedding photos, charge extra for a lavish album, a blooper reel of funny failed photos, or pictures of the reception afterwards.

When taking pictures of tourists, charge extra for a discounted admission ticket to the attraction (if you're allowed).

Sell framed photos for a small extra fee.

Find ways to add services (and value!) to customers, then offer them.

24: Sell car/boat photos

More non-techie people are selling big things like cars and boats on eBay.

With such big-ticket items, you absolutely need to have great quality photos, or they won't sell.

Brand yourself as an expert at car and boat photography, practice a lot, learn what photos customers really want and need, and deliver.

Become good at close-up photos for important details like serial numbers, and broad photos for a glimpse of the whole car.

Try not to include yourself in reflections and learn different lighting conditions and color balances for best results.

25: Zoom in on jewelry

Macro photography isn't easy, but it's crucial for jewelry sellers to do.

Buying jewelry means you have to pay a lot of attention to details, and photos illustrating said jewelry should, too.

If a jewelry seller wants to succeed online or with flyers or brochures, their pictures need to be crystal-clear and professional.

Not everyone knows how to do macro photography that works, and especially when selling online, buyers need those pictures.

Learn how to set up a cheap lightbox and use your talents to photograph jewelry collections for Etsy or eBay sellers.

26: Be competitive

Enter photo contests and competitions, and solicit feedback from the judges.

There are photo competitions held at a local, regional, national, or even international level. Such a contest might have only one winner, or many.

If it's a local contest, you probably know who's judging. This gives you the chance to solicit feedback from the judges.

Don't make it seem like you're upset you didn't win, but ask for advice on how you can win next year and what your photo didn't include or do enough of a job at conveying.

The contest prize money for major competitions is great, along with the motivation you get from winning one.

27: Shoot for cards

Playing cards, greeting cards and postcards all need good photographs.

Local photographs sell well in touristy greeting card and postcard displays, and more generic pictures might be popular too. Try to find something unique and pretty.

If you can come up with a set of 52 different pictures with the same theme – animals, reptiles, or pretty women, for example – you can publish a set of themed playing cards.

Card companies of all kinds need fresh, original photography. Even Hallmark needs to get pictures from somewhere, and you can try contacting the smaller, independent ones if you can't get an "in" at a large company.

28: Look in your own town

You should have a local newspaper or magazine that could hire you.

Some of these ideas are more geared towards big-city writers, but even small-town amateur photographers can get an "in" at a local publication.

Newspapers need freelance photographers to be on-call and cover large local events, planned or unplanned.

There are often only a few photographers on staff at a publication, so many have a budget for freelance photographers, and sometimes that money is going unused.

You can help out a local independent, whether it's a magazine or newspaper, and earn extra cash.

29: Sell your pics online

Start your own website and sell pictures directly to buyers for more profits.

Large stock photography websites have their advantages, like a dedicated advertising or marketing team that gets the website known, but you may experience more success selling your own photos.

You can easily get a photo gallery template for a website and upload watermarked, smaller-resolution photos for buyers to preview.

When they want to purchase, you can accept payment via Paypal or another payment processor, and send them the full-sized image.

Bonus: no editorial staff to reject your pics!

30: Be inspirational

You know those cheesy inspirational pictures? Someone has to take 'em.

Popular on classroom and office walls everywhere are those cheesy motivational posters with quotes that are supposed to inspire you to do your best.

There must be a reason people keep buying them... and one of the most obvious is that they often have beautiful photography.

If you can provide those photos and good quotes to match them, you can sell inspirational posters yourself. You may need to stick with smaller ones if you have a small printer, or find a website that lets you design and sell your own posters online.

Help inspire people and make money, too.

31: Sell wallpapers

With so many computers out there, there are some that still need decorating.

People love to customize, as you've no doubt figured out. Help them customize their computers with wallpapers that fit their interests.

In order for people to pay for wallpapers, they'll have to be pretty high-quality, so don't just take a bunch of random pictures and expect them to sell well.

You can make a simple blog or website to sell your wallpapers from and either go for automated delivery after payment or do it manually.

Consider selling wallpaper packs of related images – ten, twenty, fifty or more.

32: Save screens for cash

Screensavers require a bit more techie expertise, but they're fun to make.

On Windows computers, you can create screensavers of images or videos. People need screensavers to keep their monitors from burning out too early, so capitalize on this.

A screensaver of related images like bird pictures, mountain landscapes, or flowers may sell well if you have patience and time to create one.

If you don't know how, you can contact someone and partner up – you take the photos, he or she designs and releases the actual screensaver, and you split the profits.

33: Do little touch-ups

Fix red eyes, add color, or erase ugly concrete for companies and people.

If you're a photographer, you probably know Photoshop or other photo editing programs reasonably well.

Not many people do!

But nobody likes having a photo that has just a little bit wrong with it – it's annoying every time you see the picture.

Enter your photo touch-up service. Take photos that others need changed and touch them up for a small fee.

Be realistic about what you can and can't fix, however. Don't promise to erase the car if you don't know what was behind it.

34: Create ebook covers

Ebook sellers of all kinds need good, professional covers with original pics.

Contact small ebook publishers or independent writers who publish their own ebooks and ask if they would like you to take custom, original photos for their ebook covers.

If you're good at designing and laying them out, you can do the whole cover yourself; otherwise, you can provide just the photo.

There are endless possibilities: take pictures of flowers and sunny meadows for romance novels, or use details from the novel that they provide you to come up with cover ideas.

Just try not to give any major plot spoilers!

35: Sell printed clothes

When a regular t-shirt isn't enough, people want a t-shirt with local flair.

Tourists who are looking at high prices for premade t-shirts with the country's flag on them will be happy to pay less and get a handmade t-shirt with a photo of the destination they saw.

You may even be able to include a photo of them if you have an iron, printer, special printer paper, and camera on location.

You can make sweatshirts for grandmothers with family photos, parents with graduation pictures, and more.

Customized clothing will never grow old!

36: Twitter backgrounds

Try selling unique Twitter backgrounds to people who feel unique enough.

Set up shop on a blog, website or your own Twitter page and customize it with a theme based on your own photos.

Impress people with your professional design and they'll want one of their own.

It's relatively simple to make these, and you can learn how in under a day. Then, charge a small amount for a template, or a larger amount for a unique Twitter background, which you won't sell again.

For people who want to make their own unique impression on the world (or at least the part of it that Twitters), this is a worthwhile investment.

37: Website images

Headers, backgrounds, and themes; if you know the lingo, you can profit.

For those more experienced at web design, you can make your own website images and design templates for others to use.

You could sell these as cheap themes that anyone can download and get dozens or hundreds of people to download the same one, or make unique and customized one-off themes for people for a higher fee.

To do this, you should have at least a basic knowledge of Photoshop and HTML.

For a variation on this, you can design e-store banners with your photography for Etsy and eBay sellers who are less than tech-literate but need unique branding.

38: Work with publishers

Book publishers small and large need pics for their covers/contents.

While it might be hard to get an "in" at the art department of a large publisher, smaller imprints often struggle finding affordable pictures to use for their books.

Don't sell yourself short, but if you can provide these pictures for less than stock sites want, you can get a stable of imprints as clients.

Keep in constant contact with them and remind them that you're around, waiting to fulfill their next photography requests.

You may want to provide custom orders, or you can sell photos you already have.

39: Go for the small fry

Small blogs and websites need images to illustrate their sites, too.

Some people make a living off creating websites and "flipping" them, or reselling them to others. In order to do this, you need a website theme, and you can generally get a better price if it's unique.

Enter your services! You can provide unique pictures for blog owners to post in their blogs, to use as headers or theme images, and so on.

Your market of small blogs is relatively large, so even if you only sell five or ten images to a single blog, imagine the possibilities if you target just some of the millions of blogs and minor sites out there. This could mean some serious cash.

40: Cater to the parents

At every children's recital, dance, or sports game, parents want photos.

With the permission of the school, organization or group that's organizing the event, you can take your camera and a photo printer to an event and set up shop.

Take as many photos as you can, trying to take at least one individual picture of each participant, and set up shop near where the parents are hanging out to sell pictures.

For parents who forgot their cameras or aren't good at taking non-blurry shots, this is a no-brainer investment.

You can even include a business card with each purchase that has details of your contact information for future reference.

41: Network and improve

Join a photography group for privileges like group critique and discounts.

You can network with other photographer who may have great income ideas and might even purchase from you at photography groups.

These are often sponsored by camera shops or community colleges, so ask around these places and you may hear about the local group.

You get to have your pictures critiqued by others, see examples of their work, and everyone improves.

Some groups also enjoy privileges like press admission to local events or discounts at camera stores or print shops.

42: Graduation/prom pics

High school seniors and parents want to preserve those memories.

When traditional pre-prom pics are taken by parents, high school seniors run the risk of having blurry or lopsided pictures to remember their big days.

You can set up shop in your own home studio or travel to people's homes and take graduation pictures, or pictures before prom.

You may even be able to partner with a local school to offer these, or set up at a nearby location and offer free drinks or treats for kids to come by.

Try to offer multiple shots to choose from, unlike most prom photographers, and you'll win in popularity.

43: Challenge yourself

Use a list of topics and keywords to inspire you to break creative limits.

You might never think of taking pictures with the themes of "inspiration" or "home alone" – but you could sure benefit from the experience.

Opening up your mind to trying to capture new themes in your photography can have many benefits. You can improve your technical photography skills, and sometimes even get an award-winning shot out of the deal.

Try these themes to start with: $1, cuddle, destruction, beauty, tradition, a walk to remember, hearth, stylized, earth, weary.

You can look up more lists of themes online.

44: Work for hire/on-call

Be a freelancer, work on call, and earn a name for yourself by being there.

You never know when you'll need a photographer on the spur of the moment.

Well, you might not be desperately seeking one, but some people find themselves unexpectedly needing a passport photo, or a company finds out that they need a picture of the new manager for the flyer coming out tomorrow.

Place an ad in the places people might look: online boards like Kijiji, Craigslist or eBay, for example.

Offer to work-for-hire, as long as you can use the pictures in your portfolio, and always give business cards out to people you meet.

45: Blog and monetize

Explore topics you really enjoy by making paid photo blogs about them.

With Google Adsense and other affiliate programs, it's easy to monetize even a simple blog. A domain name costs $10 at the most, and hosting doesn't cost much more.

If you really like taking photos related to a topic, you can make a photo blog about it and try to monetize it through ads or affiliate products.

In fact, you can publish your own photo book (see tip 48, for example) and then link to it from your photo blogs. This is a great way to establish yourself as an expert in a photography niche, network, and make money at the same time.

46: Find TFCD models

If you and models both need more photos of them, it's a fair exchange.

TFCD transactions between photographers and models mean that the model is trading his or her time for a CD with the photos from the shoot.

This means you can get experience working with models and more images for your portfolio, while the model gets experience working with photographers and images for their portfolio. It's a win-win situation with no money involved.

If you both agree to it, you can sell images with that model for money and split the profits, or you can retain the copyrights while they're allowed to use the images for portfolio purposes only.

47: Be a travel blogger

It may seem strange but where you live, someone else wants to visit or live.

Even in small-town USA where you might not feel another person would be interested in visiting, someone in a foreign country is interested in a totally different way of life.

Such is the marvel of the internet – you can share your location with others and make money from it.

Write a travel blog, with more pictures than words if you prefer, and monetize it with sales of your own photo book, travel guide, or ads for local tourist destinations, gift stores, or companies.

If you do a lot of traveling, you can monetize this with multiple blogs or one big blog, too.

48: Publish a photo book

If you have a particular specialty, you can easily make a coffee table book.

Print-on-demand technology makes this super-easy, more so than ever before!

With a little effort and a few weeks of time, you can gather photos from one particular theme, place, or period of your life, and publish them in a coffee table photo book.

These typically aren't best-sellers, but if you have a large circle of admiring acquaintances and family members, you can make some sales.

The easiest way to sell these is to collect great photography that interests a niche audience – then you could make enough money to pay a small bill each month.

49: Keep a baby diary

Chronicle the growth of a baby from birth to a year old or more, for a fee.

You can take pictures of a baby from pregnancy to to a year old for expecting parents who really want to chronicle the life of their little one.

First-time parents are a popular audience for this type of thing (or even grandparents), and you can sometimes even recruit them from those whose weddings you photograph!

Take pictures every two weeks or month, trying to keep poses similar so they can track the growth of the baby.

Infant photography is difficult to get right, but lucrative if you know what you're doing and like kids.

50: Sell to foreign markets

If you know how to get in contact with them, they're interested in your photos.

Some photographers say that selling photos to foreign markets is even easier than selling them to national or local markets. Whatever your specialty, it may have a market in another area.

For example, Japan is a nation enamored with trains, so selling pictures of historical trains from your country may be a great way to make money and be patriotic as you advertise your country as a cool destination.

Travel photography is always popular, too; travelers in other countries may want to visit your region. Highlight unique destinations and you can easily fascinate editors or publishers in other countries.

51: Sell photos as gifts

Local gift shops are often happy to display artists' works for a commission.

If you want to get your work out there and seen, walk into local independent gift stores and small shops and ask if they'll display your work for a commission.

For every framed photo sold, they can earn a certain percentage, and you'll sold more than you would have otherwise.

Make sure you include information about yourself and contact info on the backs of photos with a removable sticker.

52: Talk to businesses

They might need you to photograph their products for websites, flyers, etc.

Small businesses like working with other small businesses, and if you're a one-person operation, you can't get much smaller than that.

Sometimes, the only barrier to online selling, greater flyer or catalog distribution, or other forms of media that a store faces is the fact that their inventory is un-photographed, and nobody has the time or knowledge to take pictures of it all.

If you can take photos of products well, you can work with small stores and help them out.

53: Restaurant photos

Take photos of restaurant menu items to help them advertise/promote.

Maybe your favorite restaurant is looking to redesign their menus or add dishes to their menus. Often, it's hard to find a food photographer who doesn't charge a fortune, and busy owners don't have time to hunt for one anyway.

If you walk in and talk to the manager, offer your services as a food photographer, and leave a portfolio of food pictures you have taken in the past, they will remember you the next time they need food pictures taken.

You can also cold call them, but it's more impressive to show up in person, so hit your close local restaurants first.

54: Visit craft fairs

Craft fairs aren't just for little old ladies. You can make a fortune at them!

People who go to craft fairs are looking to spend money on the type of things that make good gifts or decorations.

Your photos can fill a welcome niche. Take pictures of all kinds and display them – you'll quickly see which sell and which don't.

You can sell them on white matted paper, or in frames, but the former is preferable. It's easier to prepare/transport, cheaper, and allows them to choose the frame of their choice.

It's relatively inexpensive to sell these, as you only pay the cost of the print.

55: Sell on Etsy

The eBay of crafts offers a world of opportunity for artsy people everywhere.

This marketplace is a great one for photography, arguably even better than eBay because it targets buyers who are looking for the same type of stuff – handmade and directly from the artist.

You might not get rich, but you can get your name out there, promote your own website, and have a storefront with items of all sorts.

Monitor your sales to see which photos sell best and stock them accordingly.

Also, pay attention to trends and gift-giving occasions and try to target what you offer to what's popular now.

56: Get outdoors anytime

Winter or summer, take pictures of people and sell them for small change.

In the winter, you could go to the local outdoor ice rink, take cute pictures of kids skating and falling, and print them out in your car to sell to the parents.

In the summer, you can do the same thing at local parks and playgrounds.

Charge just a few dollars for each picture, but be careful parents don't think you're some weirdo. Wear a t-shirt with your photography company's name on it if possible, or carry business cards and look like a professional.

You can network with parents to get an "in" on anything from baby photos to prom pics.

57: Target the tourists

If they've been there, they want to prove it. Sell pics of destinations to tourists.

Particularly if you live somewhere that's considered to be a vacation hotspot or "exotic" and exciting, you can make a good amount doing this.

Take sets of pictures of tourists hotspots – Toronto's photos might include the CN Tower, Roger's Centre, Eaton Centre, Parliament, and harborfront, while Hollywood's set might look quite different.

Then, you can set up a stall and sell packages of pictures, either in print form or as packs of postcards, to tourists who want to remember their trips. Just be careful about street vending laws in your area and stay on the right side of the law.

58: Kids' picture books

Create/sell educational children's picture books on different topics.

Many picture books don't require that much writing (obviously), so with a bit of knowledge of the kids' educational book market, you can take a series of photos that illustrate something and publish it!

Publish-on-demand websites will help you out again here. Look up topics that are in demand, then figure out how you'd illustrate them visually.

This could be anything from a day in the life of a zoo animal to the different ecospheres that exist.

Hint: books targeting younger children don't need much writing at all, just the basics.

59: Earn at conventions

Selling photos related to the topics of conventions can pay off big-time.

Attending and setting up shop at conventions of all kinds can be profitable, if you know how to sell.

Look for topics that you can find or take photos about; for example, at a green living convention, you could sell photos of green spaces in the city or parks.

Just about every convention can be targeted with this method, if you have enough creativity to find a topic you can take photos about!

Smaller conventions may not pay off as well, but you can often network and find out more conventions that you can sell at.

60: Be an event journalist

Take and sell pictures of local events to news outlets and blogs online.

If you are always prepared for the unexpected, you can capitalize on it.

When an event happens in your area, and this can be anything from a demonstration or rally to an earthquake, document it with photos.

Then, you can sell the photos to newspapers, magazines, online news sites, blogs, and so on.

Keep the price low and they'll be snapped up, but know the value of that perfect shot, too, and don't undersell yourself.

61: Marketing companies

They always need good freelance photographers, so drop off your portfolio.

You might never get a call back, but on the other hand, you might be asked to shoot an emergency last-minute product shoot if the photographer they had lined up backs out.

Be ready to provide references or a portfolio, a detailed and honest summary of your experience and specialties, and your equipment knowledge.

If you aren't confident enough yet, build up your experience and portfolio and ask someone to look it over and tell you if you're good enough.

The work can sometimes be boring, but sometimes it's really cool and top-secret.

62: Work with writers

A picture might be worth a thousand words, but some clients want both.

Chances are good that if you have been around the photography business long, you know that photographers and writers can be like peanut butter and jelly.

Newspapers need stories, but they also need photos. Blogs need posts, but they also need photos. Books need content, but they also need photos. Sensing a theme here?

Work with a freelance writer and refer each other, or hire each other for projects and work together.

With one of you active in each of these related trades, it can be mutually beneficial.

63: Document a kid's day

A parent might love to get a day in the life of their child recorded by you.

Find parents that you know and ask if they'd be interested in a keepsake of sorts, documenting a day in the life of their child.

This can be a great annual tradition for a family, and when their kids grow older, they'll have a set of memories and a clear picture of their childhood, even the pieces they'd forgotten.

The elite and upper-class families can afford a hefty fee for this customized memento, but everyone's interested in it.

Charge accordingly; a day of your life shouldn't be cheap, either.

64: Insurance photos

It might be boring, but pictures of accidents are often quite valuable.

Accidents, broken objects, and injuries are some of the most profitable things to photograph.

If an insurance company wants documentation of a claim or disputes it, a photo can mean the difference between a family getting their money back or being bankrupted by unexpected expenses.

Depending on how you feel about the industry, it can be very lucrative and once you break in, the company will keep calling you if you do a good job.

One "in" is all you need to get started; the accidents won't stop happening!

65: Interior design proof

Take before and after photos for interior designers and charge.

Your expertise as a photographer can come in handy for interior designers. They may be able to do an amazing job redecorating, but the "after" picture won't look nearly as impressive without a "before" picture, and if they try to take both themselves, it might look terrible either way.

They need these types of photos for portfolios and idea books for future clients, while you can use them in your own portfolio and charge the designer a fee for each before and after picture set you take.

Try to make the "before" picture look dingy and terrible, and the "after" picture look model-home-style, bright and clean.

66: Take arts portfolios

Artists of all types – musicians, bands and actors – need portfolios.

While a band may need a group shot, they also need live shots for press packages and to convince record companies of their popularity.

Actors need portfolios of their different looks and roles, headshots for attaching to resumes, and broody pics to make teen girls squeal.

Even classical musicians can use some good-quality pictures of them playing at different venues.

Charge an artist a fee and help them build a diverse and top-quality portfolio so they get the gig more often.

67: Host photo tours

Help other photographers discover unique locations by hosting a tour/retreat.

Not for the antisocial or those who freak out when little details go wrong, hosting a photo tour or photographers' retreat can be immensely fun, satisfying, and even profitable.

Arrange some cool activities in the area, plan out day trips, and remember to allow extra time for everyone to get the shots of their dreams and wander off without getting left behind.

Charge enough to cover expenses and pay yourself a fair wage for the time you spend guiding people around. Show them all the nifty little spots for breakfast and dinner, and allow for free time on everyone's part, too.

68: Write a book about it

If you know photography well, write a book with what you know.

Maybe you're amazing at capturing the tiny details on a car without blowing it out of proportion, or you can get the perfect orchid pictures every time.

You can write a book, or even an instructional booklet, about what you know to help other photographers succeed, too.

Consider including resources like information on shutter speeds or apertures, bonuses, and an index to help photographers using your book in the field quickly locate what they need.

Just don't make things up or write about things you don't know very well.

69: Monitor the seasons

Every season brings new photographic opportunities; don't let them slip away.

Is it December right now? It's probably too late to sell Christmas photography. On the other hand, it's the perfect time to start thinking about Valentine's Day.

You have to start planning in advance if you want to capitalize on seasonal markets, and they can be very lucrative.

Every season has some opportunity to take, sell, or offer photos in some way. Pictures of kids at Easter egg hunts with your friend posing as the Easter Bunny could sell like hotcakes, but you need to find the costume in advance!

Think about what is two months from now.

70: Read your manual

It may be boring (or lost), but your camera manual can make you cash.

Do you know if your camera has a shutter timer that you can use to leave the shutter open for a long time?

This means you can take pictures of fireworks, stars, or Northern Lights, depending on your area.

Do you know if there's a way to reduce the brightness of your flash?

This can help minimize the number of re-takes you have to do when your portrait model blinks from the brightness.

All the little things you discover can save time, money, or both.

71: Make business cards

Increasingly, people want business cards that are as unique as they are.

The same old boring business cards don't cut it anymore. When people want a card that's as unique as they are, a photographer like you can help.

Take or find a photo that matches their looks, personality, job, the message they are trying to convey, and sell them cards.

You can partner with a printer or use websites to do this; small businesses and individuals who may not have business cards already love this.

The more unique and creative you can be, the better. Try printing it on the back of the card, with their contact info on the front.

72: Make a class book

A dance class, sports team, or the cast of a play all have devoted parents.

Making a photo book can be profitable when you partner with some organization, group or teacher who offers classes.

Parents can sign up for it in advance, or you can take pictures as you go, publish a book, and see what happens.

Include photos of every kid and don't feature on any one in particular, especially your own.

You can print them yourself as a booklet or go for a high-quality print-on-demand website where you get royalties from every book sold.

73: Take cell wallpapers

Now increasingly popular, cell wallpapers can easily be sold different ways.

Depending on how much fuss you want to go to, you can sell them yourself as downloads, from a mobile-accessible website, or contact a company and offer a partnership.

If you do contact a company, they will want a percentage of the profits, naturally. Decide if it's worth it to you, and learn what sizes of wallpapers are necessary.

You may have to do some creative cropping to get your favorite photos to fit standard cell wallpaper dimensions.

Target teens with themes like love, sadness, sports, celebs, and other evergreen ideas.

74: Stationery with a bang

Instead of bland white paper, people love writing on unique paper!

You can put photos on it that are as niche- or area-specific as you want, or use pictures that have broad appeal (cute puppies and kittens, for example).

People might not even write on your stationery, but if it looks cool enough, they'll buy it.

Remember, every age market could work: teens need paper for writing notes in school or love letters, adults need grocery lists, and older people often write letters to each other.

You can sell this as an online download or a traditional package of stationery: envelopes, paper, etc.

75: Contact recipe sites

Recipe sites online need pictures of their recipes to attract readers... yummy.

Approach recipe websites and offer to take pictures of the finished dishes. If you have a portfolio online of previous food pictures to show them, so much the better.

Small and big sites both need them, but you'll likely have more success with small ones. In exchange, they can compensate you per photo, per recipe, or even for the cost of ingredients.

You get to eat the meal and get paid, too. For any foodie, this is a dream come true.

Be warned, though... hot foods will probably be stone-cold by the time you've taken enough photos of them to sit down and eat!

76: ID/passport photos

Only if you can deal with the regulations and not get people in trouble...

In some areas, anyone can take passport photos or ID pictures as long as they adhere to regulations. In others, more stringent rules apply. Before thinking about this as a side stream of income, look up the rules where you live.

It's probably going to be a lot of repeat takes, terrible pictures that make you secretly giggle, and expressionless faces that are exactly half an inch tall if you do this.

On the other hand, people always need this service, and it's a good chance to sell them on the other services you can provide or give them your business card for future reference.

77: Company yearbooks

Yearbooks of employees – companies *are* like high schools now!

Nevertheless, someone has to take those pictures!

Even if a company doesn't do a yearbook, there's probably some kind of annual newsletter that they need a businesslike picture of their CEO for, or they want someone to take Christmas party pics.

There are lots of opportunities to help companies every year with their minor photography needs.

A few months before Christmas and the year end is a good time to approach companies and ask if they need anyone. Some might keep you on file and call you up later.

78: Do the step-by-step

It's not as much fun as the two-step: making manufacturer instructions.

Small companies that produce goods (and that's a lot of companies) need idiot-proof instructions for these goods.

If they're trying to help people put together furniture, for example, photos can be a very valuable part of a step-by-step instruction manual.

For electronics, pictures of how the back of the unit should look and where everything is plugged into may be cheaper than illustrations.

Contact manufacturers in your area and ask if they ever need this service from a freelance professional photographer.

79: Take pictures of fronts

Store-fronts, house-fronts, or waterfronts... the owners love the views.

A store might need a photo of their storefront to use in advertising (flyers, newspapers, online, etc), while a house front photo can be a good Christmas card or can feature in the family newsletter.

Taking photos of the fronts of buildings may seem dull, but you get to meet interesting people, and if you like architecture, it can be an interesting job.

It's also a great way to start breaking into the real estate photography market if you haven't already. They always need pictures of the home fronts!

Tip: learn to show depth properly.

80: Go to summer camp

Partner with a summer camp to offer pics of the kids for doting parents.

Definitely something you want to have prior permission from the camp for, you can partner up with them for mutual benefit.

Camps get to offer parents a custom picture, reassurance that their kids were safe and happy, and kids like the memories of getting photos of themselves.

Parents could pay you directly, or the camp could pay you for the service and charge the parents as they see fit.

This may mean portraits, or it may mean getting out and active with the kids, showing the parents what their little ones were occupied with over the summer.

81: Custom family books

We all have that tub of family pictures that hasn't been sorted through.

Families, particularly sentimental parents and grandparents, would probably love to have their story properly chronicled.

For an appropriate fee, you can work with the family to make a photo book of their family tree and their family's history.

This could be the immediate family only, or it could go up to grandparents and great-grandparents, depending on their records and family ties.

You could publish it privately on a print-on-demand website, or offer it to them in person when all is said and done.

82: City tourist guides

If you have any number of tourists come through your city, profit from them.

Tourists want an illustrated, detailed guide of what they're about to see and how to get there.

Publish a booklet, leaflet or flyer of some kind that shows them a walking tour, complete with map and pictures of what to look out for.

Charge them a small fee and you can sell a lot. Just make sure you comply with street vending regulations.

You can publish different booklets for different routes or parts of town, or go for a complete guide to the city.

83: Cake photography

Take pictures of, or on, cakes – work with cake decorators for this one.

Unless you're a professional cake decorator on the side, you'll want to find a cake decorator, preferably an independent one or a small company.

They need photos to print onto their cakes; you could offer some of yours. Ask them what's popular and what they often get requests for, or make a few cakes to put in their flyers and get paid per cake with your photo that's sold.

You can also take pictures *of* their cakes, useful for decorators trying to build their portfolios. This can be a very cool gig, and even a very sweet one if you're lucky!

84: Memories of events

When there's a big event in town, help people remember they attended.

Whether this is a parade or a rally, take pictures of people for a small fee and take pictures of the event itself, then sell them.

Depending on the event, you may need permission from organizers. If it's a spontaneous happening, you probably won't, however.

This can be unpredictable, and you can even have people unhappy that you took their picture, so be sensitive to people's wishes and delete the photos if they ask you to (no matter how good they are) if you want to stay happily moral.

If photos don't sell, contact newspapers.

85: Photo clipart/icons

Website designers, graphic designers, etc need icons and clipart.

Look at techies and designers of all sorts – website, graphic, or software.

Often, they need customized clipart or built-in photos as demonstrations.

You can sell your photos for use in software applications or as "default pictures" (much like the Windows and Mac OS X operating systems come with premade desktop wallpapers).

Some photos make great little icons if you downsize them and edit them properly, too.

Individuals also sometimes buy custom graphics or icons for their computers.

86: Make picture videos

This may seem to defeat the purpose of photos, but make videos from them.

If you have a lot of photos of something beautiful or of a similar theme that's popular with viewers (cats, for example), you can make a video with the photos.

Then, upload it to a paid video site where you get paid for the number of people who watch your video.

You can also upload it to Youtube and include annotations with links to your own sites as self-promotion, though you won't profit directly from it.

If you're daring, try to make it viral by making it particularly crazy, weird, alarming, or funny.

87: Furniture stores

Spaces of all kind need art, including furniture stores' setups of rooms.

In most furniture stores, there is at least one room set up, possibly more, to show what the furniture will look like when situated in the buyer's house.

They need wall-art there, too!

Prints of your photos that match the furniture decorating scheme could sell, in which case the furniture store could get a commission, or you could sell the prints to the store... or let them hang them for free, but include a phone number on each for people to call you about the art.

Find a creative way of partnering with these types of stores.

88: Make album covers

Garage-based bands everywhere are trying to make a breakout album.

Musical talent does not a photographer make, and the cover of an album represents the band itself.

Make a professional album cover for a band, and you could get famous if they do.

Take photos of the band, or work with them to figure out the artistic direction of the album and take a picture that matches it.

The correlation between music and pictures can seem very random to those who prefer the non-artistic, technical side of photography, so you might be better off avoiding this one if this describes you. Just remember, the fee for this should be small.

89: Sell email decorations

Many people like to decorate their emails, particularly older adults.

If your mother loves to insert photos of pretty things or use email templates with custom photo headers and backgrounds, you could have struck gold.

You can sell email templates to professionals, bored adults who email too much, and those who hate plain white backgrounds.

Sell them online, or through an e-store that partners with you and already does a booming business if you don't want to handle the technical hassle of walking someone through how to use it by yourself.

A small fee for each download adds up.

90: Sims/Second Life art

Crazy though it may seem, people will pay to decorate virtual space.

The avid Sims and Second Life players reading this will testify to this fact!

Some people are so fanatic about their virtual realities that they are willing to pay to decorate them.

You can convert your photos into art in most customizable virtual reality games and then sell them there, too.

Don't miss every outlet and channel of distribution when it comes to selling your photos!

Many overlook this, but it can pay off well if a few hundred people pay a dollar each.

91: Evergreen subjects

Know what sells when targeting stock/microstock photography sites.

Many people try to submit the same old boring landscapes, sunsets, or photos of their relatives.

That's not what sells.

Food items, details, generic pictures of trees and houses and computer keyboards sell better.

Some "people" photos sell, but a lot of magazines, websites and newspapers actually need item-based photos.

Experiment and look for information on your stock photography site on what actually sells the best.

92: Amateur product pics

Help teach others to take good product photos for their own eBay listings.

Some people don't want to pay others to photograph every single thing in their inventory to sell on eBay, Craigslist, etc.

Instead, they could benefit from someone who will teach them how to photograph common objects that they sell.

If you're good at photographing jewelry, cars, clothing, or other items for sale, find crafters and online businesspeople in your area who need a hand and tutor them in the fine art of product photography.

You might even include a cheatsheet of specs they should be using to take various product pics with the coaching.

93: Combine/edit photos

Teen girls want to be seen with their celeb crushes. Photoshop helps...

This can be a tremendously popular service if you offer it right.

People often need photos seriously edited, or even combined. (Just be prepared to not ask too many questions, as some requests will be odd.)

Some are even willing to pay others for it.

For a small fee, you can offer teen girls the chance to be in a photo with (insert celebrities of their choice) and watch them squeal and hand over money.

You profit, she gets to show off. Each of you ends up happy in the end!

94: School book covers

Kids everywhere cover schoolbooks with tacky paper... Save them!

You can create your own schoolbook covers with some sticky paper and a good printer.

This means you can create customized schoolbook covers and sell them in person or online.

Try some cute, generic designs like kittens and puppies, some landscapes, and "manly" designs like sports players or equipment.

You can sell them mostly in the back to school season, but any time of the year except early summer works well.

Online, Etsy, eBay, and spots where kids hang out are good places to sell from.

95: Carry your gear

Always keep your most essential stuff with you to be taken seriously.

A photographer always keeps his or her camera near at hand, and for good reason. You never know what opportunities might be literally lurking around the next corner!

If you have a bulky SLR, consider a good-quality pocket-sized camera just for the sake of having something (it's better than nothing). If you run into celebrities or a natural disaster, you can't get rich from the photos you couldn't take.

Carry model release forms if you specialize in photos of people, and business cards to hand out, because you never know when you might meet someone who needs a photographer someday.

96: Dorm decorations

Slim profit margin but a hungry market – help students decorate dorms.

You can print up posters, create customized items like doorknob hangers and removable wall vinyl clings, and more with your photos.

Set up on campus and sell during frosh week, with the permission of the college or university, of course.

Art for their walls can range from interest-based to general interest stuff like landscapes and cute animals.

Think back to what you liked in college, ask college-aged kids what's in, and print it up! You'll quickly get an idea of what sells.

97: Take pics in stores

Real estate companies like to attract customers when possible.

You can set up shop inside a store to take pictures of people, with the permission of the store owners.

Grand opening events and real estate open house days are particularly popular – imagine offering people a photo of themselves in front of the new model home, for instance.

Work with store owners to determine who needs photos taken, when, and why. They may pay you directly, or you may be able to charge the customers and give them a portion of the profits.

98: Take a class and learn

If your photography skills are limited to one trick only, upgrade your skills.

You can take a class or learn a new photography skill independently.

For example, if you've never been good at taking macro photographs, follow online tutorials or go to a photography class where you can learn it.

The barriers that most hold you back are self-imposed. Do your best to break them by educating yourself.

New knowledge can open up new opportunities and more streams of income than you ever dreamed of before.

99: Keep shooting

Take more photos all the time if you want to continue improving.

You can set a target for yourself, like taking 50 or 100 photos every weekend, uploading 30 photos to a stock site every week, or taking a roll of film every day.

The best way to improve your photography skills, and thus the amount of money you can make with your camera, is to keep shooting.

You never know just when you're going to stumble on that shot of a lifetime – and quite often, it's a complete accident.

If you think you aren't good enough to sell pictures yet, just keep practicing until you are.

100: Love it the most

To succeed in making money with photos long-term, you have to love it.

Photography isn't an easy thing to learn. There are technical terms to memorize, shutter speeds you need to know about, and you have to troubleshoot why pictures didn't turn out well.

When something goes wrong with your camera in the field, you have to fix it.

Sometimes you'll have angry people demand that you delete photos, so you have to know your rights and theirs.

It can be very profitable if you know what to do, but you have to be dedicated to your craft in order to make money for a long time.

101: Develop your style

All the masters of photography have a style; develop yours, too.

You can only find your style with a lot of work, thousands of photos, and a variety of genres tried.

You might take a lot of car photos at first, only to discover that you miss that human element and prefer portrait photography.

You might love or hate fast-paced photography, live for a cold winter photography walk or dread going outside.

Your style usually takes years to find, so give yourself plenty of chance to learn, grow, and change. Eventually, you'll find it and it won't be quite like anyone else's. Then, you will have succeeded as a photographer.

Conclusion

Is your mind racing with ideas now? Good! Grab a notepad and write them all down, because you can make a living from photography if you're creative and determined enough.

Test out new ideas, but try to focus on a few at a time so you can dedicate as much attention to your current projects as possible until they take off.

Once you have a viable stream of income, add another, and another, and so on until you have a full-time income.

Make no mistake – making a living from photography isn't easy, but if it's truly your passion, it won't be soul-sucking, either.

But however much work you have to do, remember to reward yourself with those early-morning photography walks, the cheesy sunset pictures, or whatever else you consider the "fun stuff" and can't wait to do.

That's the joy of photography.

www.ingramcontent.com/pod-product-compliance
Lightning Source LLC
Chambersburg PA
CBHW072038190526
45165CB00018B/1085